UNCOVERING THE PAST:
ANALYZING PRIMARY SOURCES

INTERNMENT CAMPS

NATALIE HYDE

Crabtree Publishing Company
www.crabtreebooks.com

Author: Natalie Hyde
Editor-in-Chief: Lionel Bender
Editors: Simon Adams, Anastasia Suen
Content review: Janine Deschenes
Proofreader: Laura Booth,
  Wendy Scavuzzo
Project coordinator: Petrice Custance
Design and photo research: Ben White
Production: Kim Richardson
**Production coordinator and
  prepress technician:** Ken Wright
Print coordinator: Katherine Berti
Consultant: Amie Wright,
  The New York Public Library

Cover photo: BKGD: Newspaper article
  from Rocky Shimpo, "Camp Disturbance
  Pending."
Cover Foreground: Lone Pine, California.
  Evacuees of Japanese ancestry arrive here
  by train and await buses for Manzanar.
Title Page: Sign at Manzanar
  Internment camp.

Photographs and reproductions:
Cover: Wikimedia (U.S. National Archives and Records Administration)
Alaska State Archives, Historical Collections: 31 Top Rt (Evelyn Butler/George Dale, asl_p306_1040), 31 Btm Rt (Evelyn Butler/George Dale, asl_p306_2266); Library and Archives Canada: 6 (Tak Toyota/C–046350), 20–21 (PA–170620), 38–39 (Jack Long/National Film Board of Canada Photothèque/PA–142853); Corbis Images: 4–5 (Corbis), 26–27 Mid (Horace Bristol), 29 (Bettmann); Getty Images: 7 (Justin Sullivan), 30–31 (Photoquest), 37 (Bettmann), 39 (Sacramento Bee), 40–41 (Miami Herald), 41 Top Rt (Roberto Machado Noa); Library of Congress: 1 (LC–USZ62–75794), 22 (LC–USF34–016130–C), 23 (LC–DIG–ppmsca–07746), 24 (LC–USZ62–23602), 27 Rt (LC–USF34–072309–D), 28–29 (LC–USZ62–89914), 30, 32, 34, 36 Top Left (Icon) (LC–DIG–pppps–00246), 32 Btm (LC–USZ62–117148), 34–35 (LC–DIG–pppps–00368), 35 (LC–DIG–pppps–00252); Scholastic Canada Ltd: 14 (Scholastic Canada Ltd); Shutterstock.com: 3 (Laurin Rinder), 4, 6, 8, 10, 12, 14 Top Left (Icon) (Zack Frank), 16, 18 Top Left (Icon) (Lowe Llaguno), 20, 22, 24, 26, 28 Top Left (Icon) (photogal), 38, 40 Top Left (Icon) (William Silver); Sing Out Louise Productions: 15 (Sing Out Louise Productions); Topfoto: 8–9, 11, 12, 19, 25 Middle Lft, 28, 33, 36 (The Granger Collection); 16–17 (World History Archive); 18 (Ann Ronan Picture Library/Heritage images); 21 (Ann Ronan Picture Library/Heritage images); University of Washington Libraries Special Collections: 10 (UW37336), 13 (UW14752a), 25 Btm Rt (UW37337), 27 Btm (UW37338) **Map:** Stefan Chabluk

This book was produced for
Crabtree Publishing Company
by Bender Richardson White

Library and Archives Canada Cataloguing in Publication

CIP available at the Library and Archives Canada

Library of Congress Cataloging-in-Publication Data

Names: Hyde, Natalie, 1963- author.
Title: Internment camps / Natalie Hyde.
Description: New York : Crabtree Publishing Company, 2016.
  | Series: Uncovering the past: analyzing primary sources |
  Includes bibliographical references and index. |
  Audience: Ages 10-14. | Audience: Grade 4 to 6.
Identifiers: LCCN 2016022627 (print) | LCCN 2016025885 (ebook)
  | ISBN 9780778728603 (reinforced library binding) |
  ISBN 9780778728627 (pbk.) |
  ISBN 9781427118417 (electronic HTML)
Subjects: LCSH: Japanese Americans--Evacuation and relocation,
  1942-1945--Juvenile literature. | World War, 1939-1945--Japanese
  Americans--Juvenile literature. | Japanese--Canada--History--
  20th century--Juvenile literature.
Classification: LCC D769.8.A6 H93 2016 (print) | LCC D769.8.A6
  (ebook) | DDC 940.53/170973--dc23
LC record available at https://lccn.loc.gov/2016022627

Crabtree Publishing Company
www.crabtreebooks.com   1-800-387-7650

Printed in Canada/072016/PB20160525

Published in Canada
Crabtree Publishing
616 Welland Ave.
St. Catharines, ON
L2M 5V6

Published in the United States
Crabtree Publishing
PMB 59051
350 Fifth Avenue, 59th Floor
New York, NY 10118

Published in the United Kingdom
Crabtree Publishing
Maritime House
Basin Road North, Hove
BN41 1WR

Published in Australia
Crabtree Publishing
3 Charles Street
Coburg North
VIC, 3058

UNCOVERING THE PAST

THE PAST COMES ALIVE

"History cannot give us a program for the future, but it can give us a fuller understanding of ourselves, and of our common humanity, so that we can better face the future."

Robert Penn Warren (1905–1989), American poet

ANALYZE THIS

Many more Japanese were interned in North America during World War II than Germans and Ukrainians. Why was it easier to target the Japanese than people of European descent?

War is always a time ruled by "us against them" **mentality**. Because of this, entire groups of **civilians** in wartime can be seen as "enemies." Governments decide these people need to be kept separate from the general population. They **confine** them in areas called **internment** or **concentration camps**. During **World War II**, people were **interned** based on their religion or nationality. In North America, both Canada and the United States interned people of German, Italian, and Japanese descent in camps. In this book, we are focusing on the internment of Japanese Americans and Japanese Canadians.

After a war ends, many people want to forget the terrible things that happened. They might feel regret for their actions. Memories might be too painful. No one wants to believe they acted as horribly as the enemy they were fighting. But it is important that we look at the past.

The past is time that has gone by. It can be things that happened a few years ago or things that happened thousands of years ago. Important events, even terrible events, show us the truth about ourselves and others. The laws and rights we have in place today are a result of studying the past to see how we can change, grow, and hopefully improve.

Looking back at the **evidence** of internment camps during World War II helps us to understand how easily fear and hate influence our actions. We can see the seeds of **racism** and **discrimination**. We can also see human kindness and forgiveness.

DEFINITIONS

The past can be defined in different ways:

A decade is 10 years, a century is 100 years, and a millennium is 1,000 years.

A generation is all the people born and living at the same time, such as the postwar generation (those born after World War II).

An era is a period of time with a certain characteristic, such as the Mackenzie King era (the time when William Mackenzie King was prime minister of Canada).

An age is a long period of time, such as the Age of Exploration (15th to 17th centuries) when explorers from Europe found new lands.

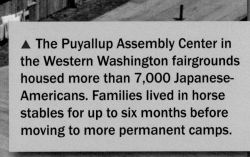

▲ The Puyallup Assembly Center in the Western Washington fairgrounds housed more than 7,000 Japanese-Americans. Families lived in horse stables for up to six months before moving to more permanent camps.

HOW DO WE LEARN ABOUT THE PAST?

We look for evidence. Everything that happens in the world leaves a trace. Sometimes these traces are created by nature, such as fossils. Other times they are created by humans, such as reports or paintings.

So where can we find evidence to study? Documents, images, and **artifacts** are found in libraries, archives, museums, and private collections. There they are catalogued and stored so that people can access them. Sometimes evidence is **preserved** by accident. Magazines might be left, forgotten in an attic. Old tools and machines might be stored in a barn. Newspapers might be used inside walls for insulation or to pack old dishes. Some evidence remains in the memories of people who experienced the event. Listening to their

PERSPECTIVES

Look at the way Japanese-Canadians were transported to the internment camps in the interior of British Columbia. How do you think they felt being loaded onto open trucks? Do you think they were being treated respectfully?

▼ The relocation of Japanese-Canadians to internment camps happened so quickly that it was easy for friends, family, and possessions to be separated or lost.

"I hereby authorize and direct the Secretary of War ... to prescribe military areas in such places and of such extent as he or the appropriate Military Commander may determine, from which any or all persons may be excluded, and with respect to which, the right of any person to enter, remain in, or leave shall be subject to whatever restrictions the Secretary of War or the appropriate Military Commander may impose in his discretion."

President Franklin D. Roosevelt, February 19, 1942

ANALYZE THIS

As time goes by, the amount of evidence on the creation, use, and conditions of the internment camps lessens. In what ways can evidence be "lost" over time?

interviews and reading their **memoirs** are a way for us to see the event through their eyes.

Historians study, research, and write about the past. They are usually experts in the history of a certain period in time, place, or event. Their job includes collecting and analyzing materials. They need to remain **objective**. Roger Daniels is a historian on Japanese-American internment. He lectures and writes books on immigration and internment.

Historians researching internment camps face some challenges. Because these camps were operated by the government, some records may not be available to the public. Other documents may be destroyed or hidden, as people may not have wanted to admit their actions at that time. Others involved may not want to be interviewed, as they do not want to relive such a painful and distressing time of their lives.

▼ The Hollywood Protective Association encouraged their members to "Keep Hollywood White." They wanted the Japanese to only buy homes in the Little Tokyo area of town and stay out of their neighborhoods.

TYPES OF EVIDENCE

*"He (Nathan Van Patten) collected items that might not have seemed valuable at the time, like a poster from the camp library, but that sort of **ephemera** really speaks the daily lives of the internees."*

Courtney Sato, curator

Evidence of the past is called **source material**. It is created every time something is preserved, recorded, written down, photographed, or when paintings or stories are made. Each time you snap a picture, blog about your day, or fill in a form, you are creating source material, too. Source material is important because it lets us investigate a person, place, or event and draw our own conclusions, rather than relying on other people's **interpretations** of the past.

Because it is so valuable to our knowledge of the past, it is important that source material is preserved. Old newspapers, magazines, documents, and photographs are sometimes copied onto film. This way, researchers can look at them without damaging the original with heat, light, or sweat. Other source materials are kept behind glass that restricts damaging sunlight. Displays can also have a steady temperature to help slow the aging process. Other items are so valuable that they are stored in vaults or archives for safekeeping. Access to these items is tightly controlled to prevent damage.

There is a good amount of source material about World War II internment camps. The war was in the recent past when we already had cameras and recording equipment that captured images and speeches. The governments involved in the conflict and responsible for the camps produced records, files, and memos that have remained. Also many articles, reports, and novels have been written during and about life in these camps.

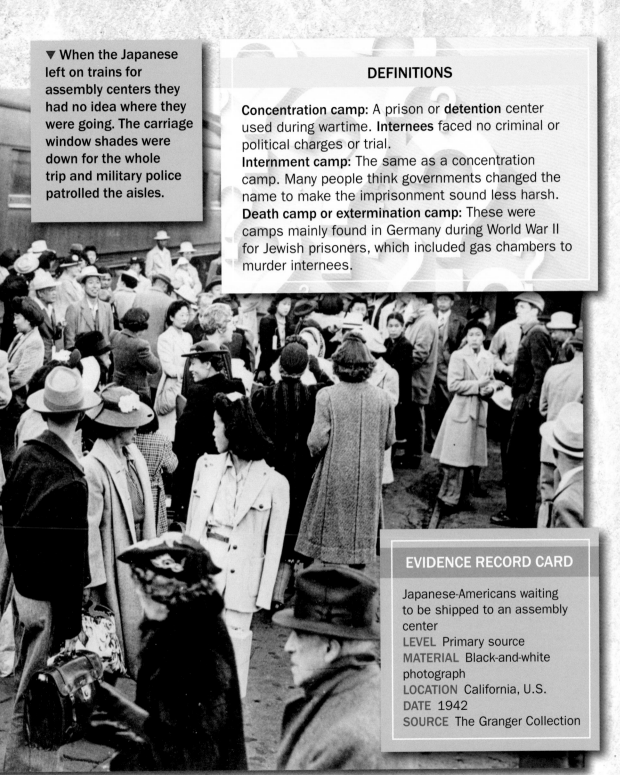

▼ When the Japanese left on trains for assembly centers they had no idea where they were going. The carriage window shades were down for the whole trip and military police patrolled the aisles.

DEFINITIONS

Concentration camp: A prison or **detention** center used during wartime. **Internees** faced no criminal or political charges or trial.

Internment camp: The same as a concentration camp. Many people think governments changed the name to make the imprisonment sound less harsh.

Death camp or extermination camp: These were camps mainly found in Germany during World War II for Jewish prisoners, which included gas chambers to murder internees.

EVIDENCE RECORD CARD

Japanese-Americans waiting to be shipped to an assembly center
LEVEL Primary source
MATERIAL Black-and-white photograph
LOCATION California, U.S.
DATE 1942
SOURCE The Granger Collection

HISTORICAL SOURCES

PRIMARY SOURCES

Source material can be divided into two types: **primary sources** and **secondary sources**. Primary sources come directly from people experiencing something. They are direct evidence of an event. Primary sources can be things that you can read, see, and/or hear.

Primary written sources can include:

- Letters: Notes written on paper and sent between people
- Journals: Entries in a book about a trip or a special event
- Lyrics: The words to a song
- Advertisements: Descriptions of services or items offered for sale
- Telegrams: Messages sent by signals over a wire and then written down
- Diaries: Personal thoughts kept in a notebook
- Transcripts: Written copies of interviews, meetings, or speeches
- Blogs: Journals posted online
- Social media: Posts and updates on public sites online

ANALYZE THIS

Take a close look at the postcard below. It was written by a Japanese internee, Harry Masuto. Many thought that Japanese people were lower class citizens. Do you think this postcard makes Harry Masuto sound like an average American? What details back up your opinion?

▼ Harry Masuto sent this postcard to James Sakamoto. Internees not only wrote letters and postcards, but also ordered items from catalogues or from the companies that placed ads in camp newspapers through the mail.

June 16, 1942
WCCA North Portland

Dear Jimmy;

Just a line to let you and the rest know that all of us are down here in Portland. Everthing is going O.K. and hope the same to you.

Working with Newton, Howard, Fraces Maeda and the rest of the bunch and am getting along fine for as you known we all have worked together before.

Spud and Sumis are in the Eastern Oregon beet fields and are coming back soon. They headed a group of volunteers immediately on their arrival. They like it in the beet filds.

If you should want to contact anyone from Wash. just adress it the above. adressMaybe we will be together before long. We are certainly having lots of rain these days.

Sincerly Harry Masuto.

With governments involved in the **evacuation** and detention of "enemy aliens," there was a huge paper trail left behind. Libraries and archives in the United States hold naval dispatches, copies of the Civil Exclusion Order forcing the evacuation of citizens, and the records of the War Relocation Authority. Libraries and archives in Canada hold copies of the War Measures Act in Canada, lists of Japanese deported to Japan, and the medical records of German prisoners held in Canada, as well as letters and diaries of internees.

There are many personal primary source documents as well. Many of the internees wrote letters to relatives or kept journals and diaries. Businesses and organizations also produced primary source material in petitions, notices, and/ or the minutes of their meetings relating to "enemy aliens" in their communities.

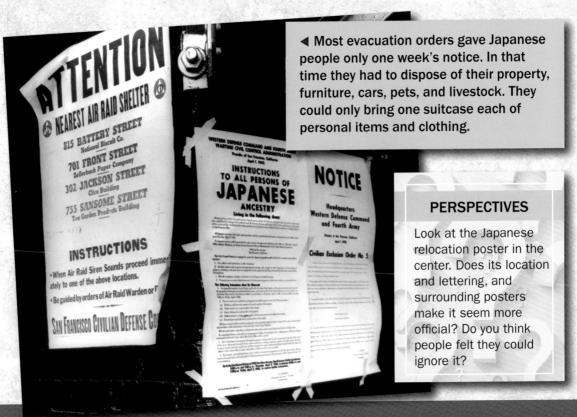

◀ Most evacuation orders gave Japanese people only one week's notice. In that time they had to dispose of their property, furniture, cars, pets, and livestock. They could only bring one suitcase each of personal items and clothing.

PERSPECTIVES

Look at the Japanese relocation poster in the center. Does its location and lettering, and surrounding posters make it seem more official? Do you think people felt they could ignore it?

"It's just change, going from living in a home, into a camp. The first experience of losing our freedom. Knowing what it was like, because there was a searchlight on top of the guard towers, that would scan the whole area. If you went to the bathroom at night, that light followed you. I think it's just the change, of all those things I had to experience, more than I really want to remember."

Bess K. Chin, former internee, April 21, 2005

VISUAL EVIDENCE

Primary sources can also be **visual** items. Visual items are images made by people or technology. Before modern times, images of events, places, and people were captured by painters. They give us evidence of the past by showing us the traditions, fashions, and reactions to events long ago. Artists today still create primary visual sources when they draw, illustrate, or create political cartoons.

Photographs and video are powerful sources of information. Images and movies can create emotion in the viewer, as well as deliver facts about uplifting, tragic, or exciting events. Some images can even become a symbol of an event. The famous photograph of Neil Armstrong walking on the moon,

for instance, symbolizes the amazing achievement of man **conquering** space.

Visual primary sources can include:
- Photographs: Images created on film and printed on paper or disk
- Paintings: Images made on canvas with paint
- Video and movies: Moving images recorded by cameras
- Billboards: Large outdoor boards showing advertisements for items or services
- Maps: Diagrams of a region or area
- Political cartoons: Images drawn by an illustrator to make a point, with or without words
- Posters: Images printed on large sheets of paper with or without words

EVIDENCE RECORD CARD

Cartoon by Dr. Seuss
LEVEL Primary source
MATERIAL Political cartoon
PUBLICATION New York City Newspaper *PM*
DATE February 13, 1942
SOURCE The Granger Collection

► This cartoon reflected the fear many people had that the Japanese on the Pacific Coast of the United States were spies, working for Japan.

Photographs are some of the most powerful primary visual sources for internment camps during World War II. Through the eyes of the camera we can see the effect of being told you were now an enemy of your country and must take only what you can carry in one suitcase. Photographs show the cruel conditions in Jewish concentration camps in Germany. They also show the relief and joy on the faces of internees when they are freed.

Auditory sources are another type of primary source material. This is source material that you can hear. Recordings of speeches or interviews are auditory sources, as are music or songs. Interviews with former Japanese or Jewish internment camp residents are available online. Auditory sources let us hear people's memories of events they experienced in their own voices. Emotions such as fear, sadness, and relief can be heard in how they speak or even cry. Music is a unique way of sharing information and memories. Rap songs such as "Kenjii" by Fort Minor tell the story of one Japanese-American and how his life was affected by the policy to intern "enemy aliens."

▼ Frank Kunishige's Alien's Indefinite Leave card allowed him to travel to another location in Idaho, but only along the most direct route.

WRA-138

UNITED STATES WAR RELOCATION AUTHORITY
ALIEN'S INDEFINITE LEAVE

THIS IS TO CERTIFY THAT
Mr. Asakichi Kunishige
AN ALIEN OF JAPANESE NATIONALITY RESIDING
Minidoka
WITHIN ____ RELOCATION AREA, IS ALLOWED
TO LEAVE SUCH AREA ON Jan. 5, 44 ____ 19 ____ TO TRAVEL TO
Twin Falls, Idaho

TRAVEL TO THE ABOVE DESTINATION HAS BEEN PERMITTED BY THE DEPARTMENT OF JUSTICE. ANY TRAVEL THEREFROM MAY TAKE PLACE ONLY WITH THE PERMIS-
Boise, Idaho

SION OF THE UNITED STATES ATTORNEY AT ____. ANY SUBSEQUENT TRAVEL MAY TAKE PLACE ONLY WITH THE PERMISSION OF THE UNITED STATES ATTORNEY OF THE JUDICIAL DISTRICT INCLUDING THE NEW POINT OF DEPARTURE, SUBJECT TO SUCH PERMISSION, SUBJECT TO THE TERMS OF THE REGULATIONS OF THE WAR RELOCATION AUTHORITY RELATING TO THE ISSUANCE OF LEAVE FOR DEPARTURE FROM A RELOCATION AREA AND SUBJECT TO ANY SPE-CIAL CONDITIONS OR RESTRICTIONS SET FORTH ON THE REVERSE SIDE HEREOF. THE HOLDER IS ENTITLED TO LEAVE OF INDEFINITE DURATION FROM SUCH RELO-CATION AREA

23550 R. S. Davidson
(PROJECT DIRECTOR)

AMERICAN BANK NOTE CO.

SECONDARY SOURCES

Information about the past can also be found in secondary sources. Secondary sources are one step farther away from the actual event and are usually created long after the time the event happened by people who were not there. Sometimes this source material is created by looking at, or **evaluating**, primary sources such as news reports and magazine articles. Novels that are written about a certain time period or paintings created about a moment in history are secondary sources.

Secondary sources can include:
- Novels: Stories that are fictional
- Paintings: Images on canvas that were created long after an event
- Magazine articles: Writing that focuses on a topic
- Textbooks: Books containing facts and figures

- Encyclopedias: A set of books or websites that give a little information on many subjects
- Movies: Fictional stories on film

There were many magazine articles written about the Japanese internees in the 1940s. Some were titled "The Problem People" and "Spies on the West Coast." The messages in the articles helped fuel the fear of "enemy aliens" and **justified** in many people's minds the necessity of the camps. Novels set in Japanese internment camps help readers identify with the confusion, anger, and

ANALYZE THIS

Do you think the secondary sources mentioned in this chapter have more **bias** than primary sources? Why or why not?

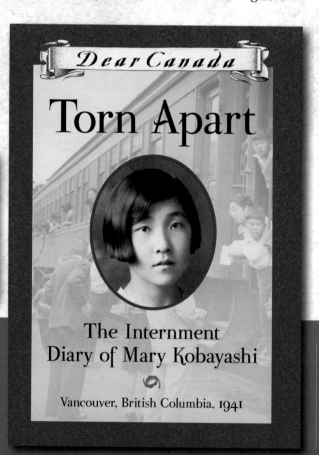

Dear Canada

Torn Apart

The Internment Diary of Mary Kobayashi

Vancouver, British Columbia, 1941

▶ Author Susan Aihoshi based her novel on stories from her own ancestors who were interned at the New Denver camp in British Columbia's Slocan Valley.

fear of people singled out during wartime. *The Bracelet* is the story of Emi, who is sent to a camp in Montana and loses the bracelet of her friend she left behind. In *Torn Apart: The Internment Diary of Mary Kobayashi*, Mary and her two sisters are separated from their parents and sent to different camps in the interior of British Columbia.

Plays based on historical events are also secondary sources. Actor George Takei, famous for his role on the TV series *Star Trek*, was once interned at Rohwer camp in Arkansas with his family. His time there is the inspiration for the musical *Allegiance*, in which he also stars.

PERSPECTIVES

If you study the theater poster for *Allegiance*, set in the Heart Mountain Relocation Center, what would be your impression of internment camps?

▼ While most people agree that *Allegiance* shines a light on a dark topic, others criticize the exaggeration of violence in the camp.

A NATION DIVIDED. ONE FAMILY, INDIVISIBLE

ALLEGIANCE

A NEW MUSICAL INSPIRED BY A TRUE STORY

LEA **SALONGA**   GEORGE **TAKEI**

"*Emi ran to the door when she heard the doorbell. Maybe, she thought, a messenger from the government would be standing there, tall and proper and buttoned into a uniform. Maybe he would tell them it was all a mistake, that they didn't have to go to camp after all.*"

Yoshiko Uchida, a detainee

INTERPRETATION

"Facts are stubborn things; and whatever may be our wishes . . . they cannot alter the state of facts and evidence."

President John Adams, second president of the United States

When looking at both primary and secondary sources, historians look for **accurate** accounts of what happened. But not all sources are objective. Some sources will slant in favor of one point of view over another. This is called bias. Bias is expected because each person's version of what happened depends on their background, **culture**, and experience. It is important for researchers and historians to recognize bias in source material.

Historians use the **Bias Rule** when reading source material. The Bias Rule says that historians should think about each piece of evidence **critically**. They should also always take into account the creators' point of view. Lastly, each piece should be crosschecked and compared with other documents.

Researchers need to keep in mind that source material about Japanese internment camps often shows a bias. Looking at many different points of view gives a balanced understanding of events. A sign in a store window reading "Japs Go Home" would have a different meaning for the Japanese being deported than for those Americans who had family members killed fighting in Japan.

Documents from the government show the Japanese living in North America as a threat. Language in these files describes "enemy aliens," "yellow peril," and "problem people." Letters, journals, and interviews from Japanese who were interned show a different side of the event. There was injustice as they were taken from their homes and had their property sold without their consent.

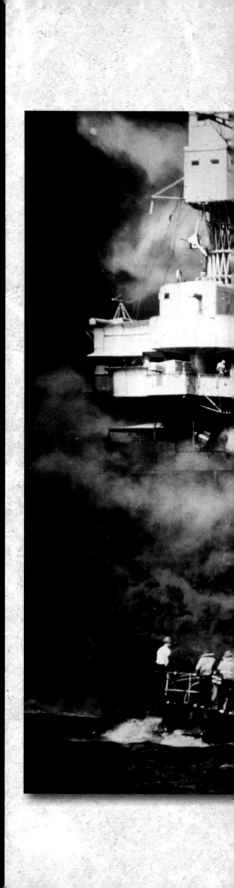

PERSPECTIVES

If you saw this photograph of the Japanese attack on Pearl Harbor in a 1941 newspaper, do you think it would affect your attitude toward the internment of the Japanese people in the United States? Why or why not?

◀ On December 7, 1941, Japanese planes attacked the U.S. naval base at Pearl Harbor in Hawaii. In just two hours they destroyed almost 20 ships and more than 300 airplanes, and caused the deaths of more than 2,000 soldiers and sailors.

FINDING RELIABLE SOURCES

When looking at source documents, historians also keep the **context** of the event in mind. Context is the set of circumstances or facts that surround a certain event or situation. By understanding the context the source was created in, a researcher can think more critically about the meaning of the evidence.

The context of internment camps is that they were used during wartime. At this time people were frightened, angry, and afraid of "the enemy." There was a lot of **patriotic** feeling for their homeland. There was an urgent need to protect borders and defend their culture and their future. Camps in North America first held people who originated from Canada's first enemy: the Germans and their supporters. The bombing of Pearl Harbor was the context behind the opening of camps for people of Japanese background. Looking at the context of World War II can help researchers understand behavior that might seem strange at another time in history.

Historians use the Time and Place Rule to help them figure out how reliable source material

▼ **The United States declared war on Japan on December 8, 1941, the day after the bombing of Pearl Harbor.**

Seventy-seventh Congress of the United States of America;
At the First Session

Begun and held at the City of Washington on Friday, the third day of January, one thousand nine hundred and forty-one

JOINT RESOLUTION

Declaring that a state of war exists between the Imperial Government of Japan and the Government and the people of the United States and making provisions to prosecute the same.

Whereas the Imperial Government of Japan has committed unprovoked acts of war against the Government and the people of the United States of America : Therefore be it

Resolved by the Senate and House of Representatives of the United States of America in Congress assembled, That the state of war between the United States and the Imperial Government of Japan which has thus been thrust upon the United States is hereby formally declared; and the President is hereby authorized and directed to employ the entire naval and military forces of the United States and the resources of the Government to carry on war against the Imperial Government of Japan; and, to bring the conflict to a successful termination, all of the resources of the country are hereby pledged by the Congress of the United States.

Speaker of the House of Representatives.

H A Wallace
Vice President of the United States and President of the Senate.

Approved
Dec. 8 1941 4.10 p.m. E.S.T.

Franklin D Roosevelt

> "I was leaving the breakfast table when the ship's siren for air defense sounded. Having no anti-aircraft battle station, I paid little attention to it. Suddenly I heard an explosion. I ran to the port door leading to the quarterdeck and saw a bomb strike a barge of some sort alongside the NEVADA, or in that vicinity. The marine color guard came in at this point saying we were being attacked. I could distinctly hear machine gun fire."
>
> Marine Corporal E.C. Nightingale, stationed at Pearl Harbor

might be. This rule states that the closer in time to the event that the evidence was created, the better the source will be.

From most reliable to less reliable:

- Direct traces of an event, such as remains of internment camps
- Firsthand accounts created at the time the event occurred, such as photographs taken at the time, speeches recorded live, diaries written as events happened
- Firsthand accounts created after the event, such as memoirs written by former internees
- Accounts created after the event by people who did not witness it themselves but use interviews or evidence from that time, such as paintings created today of what life in the camps might have looked like.

PERSPECTIVES

Look closely at this 1942 poster. What details in the illustration of the Japanese soldier encourage viewers to feel mistrust and hate for the enemy?

▶ Propaganda is biased communication that helps sway people's opinion. In World War II anti-Japanese posters were designed to increase support for the war by creating hatred for the enemy.

WWII INTERNMENT CAMPS

"I am for the immediate removal of every Japanese on the West Coast to a point deep in the interior."

Henry McLemore, columnist, Hearst newspapers

ANALYZE THIS

Only two Canadian internment camps during World War I —Spirit Level and Vernon—were set up for families. What facilities would a camp set up for families need? Does this camp look like a suitable place for children? What are your reasons?

Internment camps, also called concentration camps, were not an invention of World War II. They had been used throughout history during wartime to hold and control the enemy. The conditions in these camps varied from harsh to deadly. Often prisoners were made to work themselves to death on railways, in the fields, or in the camps.

During **World War I**, Canada interned Germans, Ukrainians, and Bulgarians. Many were put to work creating Canada's national parks. In the United States, German-Americans shared space with German merchant sailors who were in American ports when war was declared.

In World War II, the use of internment camps around the world not only increasd, but in some areas become something far more **sinister** and deadly. The **Nazi**-led German government created camps for Jewish people and others it considered undesirables with gas chambers to murder internees. Millions of people died in these **death camps**. The British, French, and Italians all detained people who originated from the countries they were fighting.

In North America during World War II, Canada and the United States both interned Germans, Italians, and Japanese. The United States also relocated the **Aleuts** to internment camps in southern Alaska. For both Canada and the United States, the largest internment camps were for the Japanese. They were located mostly on or near the Pacific Coast, where most Japanese lived.

◄ During the Boer War in South Africa of 1899–1902, British forces kept Boer (Dutch-speaking settlers) women and children in a concentration camp. This represented the first use of the internment of civilians in camps in wartime.

▲ During World War I in Canada, mostly Ukrainian and German men were interned but not women or children. Many had no choice but to follow the men into the camps because they had nowhere else to live and no money to live on.

LIMITING RIGHTS

Years before World War II broke out, fear and racism toward the Japanese in North America had already begun. A lack of jobs and opportunities in Japan at the time led to the Japanese leaving their country to look for a better life in North America. Soon after Japanese **immigrants** began arriving, governments put laws in place to limit how many Japanese could immigrate and what rights they had.

Laws in Canada stated that these new immigrants could not vote, practice law, or earn more than the minimum wage. In the United States, they couldn't vote, buy land, or run for political office. So the Issei (first-generation Japanese immigrants) had to work harder and longer hours to make a living wage. People didn't mind immigrants when they worked for really low wages at jobs no one else wanted to do. Once

ANALYZE THIS

What do you think the Asiatic Exclusion League was hoping would happen by limiting the rights of Japanese immigrants? Do you think it was effective? Why or why not?

▼ Farmworkers were paid by how many bushels they picked. Japanese workers could earn twice the pay of others because they were fast and efficient.

"Please make sure that you are not buying Japanese-made goods, otherwise you are helping the Japanese to slaughter our people, bomb our cities and colleges."

Poster from The Young China Club

they were doing well, people **accused** them of stealing jobs from white workers. Organizations like the Asiatic Exclusion League (AEL) worked to stop immigration from Asia completely.

The minutes of the meetings of the AEL are available online and in the University of Illinois library. These documents give researchers an in-depth look at the beliefs and actions of this group.

As World War II began, suspicion against immigrants got worse. Racist organizations tried to convince people that Japan was smuggling an army into Canada. In the United States rumors spread that the Japanese were working as spies and that Japanese fishermen in both countries were mapping the coastline for a Japanese invasion.

We can see this attitude in war posters from the United States that show an exaggerated face of a Japanese soldier listening in to a conversation, and then warns: "Open trap make happy Jap." Even the children's book author Dr. Seuss contributed to these rumors. He drew political cartoons showing the Japanese in the United States lining up for explosives to help a Japanese attack (See page 12).

▼ "Enemy aliens" are any natives or citizens of a nation that a country is fighting. This cartoon shows that during World War I Americans considered Germans to be an "enemy alien" hovering over them.

ENEMY ALIEN MENACE

EVIDENCE RECORD CARD

Cartoon entitled "The Breath of the Hun"
LEVEL Primary source
MATERIAL Pen-and-ink drawing
PUBLICATION *New York Herald* newspaper
DATE March 28, 1918
SOURCE Library of Congress Prints and Photographs

THE COMING OF WAR

Pressure from anti-immigrant groups increased as the war went on. They convinced the governments of both Canada and the United States to tighten **restrictions** on the Japanese. On September 1, 1939, Canada entered World War II. Two days later Canada brought in the Defence of Canada Regulations. These security measures gave the country the right to send groups to internment camps, ban newspapers, and even control the right to free speech.

One year later, in 1940, even though it was not at war yet, the United States brought in the Alien Registration Act. It forced Mexicans, Japanese, Chinese, Poles, Finns, Germans, British, and even Canadians to register. "Aliens" had to complete a form and have their fingerprints taken. More than 4.7 million people registered. The government assured them it was for their protection. However, after the United States declared war in 1941, the government used the information to arrest almost 3,000 registered aliens and intern thousands more.

Immigrants, especially the Japanese, were already targeted with racism at the

▼ The Japanese-American owner of this store posted this sign the day after the attack on Pearl Harbor. He was still evacuated.

"It shall be the duty of every alien now or hereafter in the United States, who (1) is fourteen years of age or older, (2) has not been registered and fingerprinted under section 30, and (3) remains in the United States for thirty days or longer, to apply for registration and to be fingerprinted before the expiration of such thirty days."

The Alien Registration Act of 1940 (The Smith Act)

beginning of the war, but things got much worse with the bombing of Pearl Harbor. Japan had declared war, and hatred and fear of Japanese immigrants in North America skyrocketed. Every Japanese person was suspected of spying or helping Japan. It was easy to convince governments that they had to be locked away because they were a threat.

Canada used the War Measures Act to legally remove Japanese-Canadians from the coast and intern them in camps. In the United States, President Roosevelt signed Executive Order 9066, which allowed officials to begin excluding Japanese-Americans from the West Coast and imprisoning them inland.

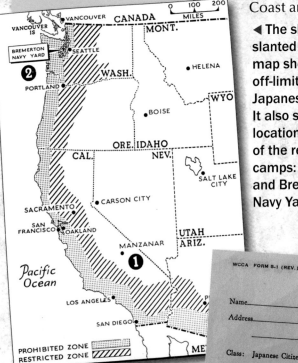

◀ The shaded and slanted lines on this map show areas off-limits to Japanese interns. It also shows the locations of two of the relocation camps: Manzanar and Bremerton Navy Yard.

WCCA FORM 5-1 (REV.)

ROUTING AND CONTROL SLIP

Name_____

Address_____

_____

Case Number_____

Sex: Male ☐   Female ☐

Number in Family_____

Class: Japanese Citizen ☐   Japanese Alien ☐

SERVICES REQUESTED
☐ Social Service
☐ Property (Farm Security)
☐ Property (Federal Reserve)
☐ Employment Service
☐ Other: (specify)

SERVICES RENDERED
☐ Social Data Registration
☐ Property Form
☐ Medical Examination
☐ Travel Permit: Issued ☐   Authorized ☐
Remarks_____

Date_____

Per_____

▶ This Routing and Control Slip was a way for the U.S. government to keep track of interned Japanese families.

EVACUATION

Evacuation notices were posted in Japanese neighborhoods and businesses all along the Pacific Coast. With very little time to prepare, families had to close up their homes, sell or put belongings in storage, and pack. Canadian internees were told the government would hold their properties for them. They were told to only bring linens, toilet articles, and extra clothing. They also had to bring forks, knives, spoons, plates, bowls, and cups for each family member. Lastly, if they still had room in their one suitcase, they could bring personal items such as books or toys for the children. Pets had to be left behind.

Families who didn't report to the meeting areas or train stations were taken **forcibly** from their homes. When they arrived they were given a number. Many felt they were being stripped of their identity. The trains were crowded and noisy. People were frightened and had no idea where they were going. Because the decision to evacuate the Japanese happened quickly, the camps were not ready. Evacuees first had to go to assembly centers. These were **temporary** holding areas put together in a hurry. In Canada, many Japanese were sent to Hastings Park in Vancouver, where they were given animal stalls as living quarters. The families were only separated by a piece of cloth draped from the top bunk of bunk beds.

In the United States, racetracks and fairgrounds became assembly centers. At Santa Anita Park racetrack, flooring had been laid down over manure stained boards. When it got hot, the smell of horse manure drove most people outside. There was a lack of proper

PERSPECTIVES

Look at the features of this settlement in the photograph. Does this look like a camp, a city, or a prison? How do you think the people living there felt? What details in the image influenced your answer?

▶ Internment camps were purposely set up in areas far away from other cities and surrounded by harsh landscapes. This was to keep contact with the outside world and all possibilities of escape to an absolute minimum.

"You, who deal in lifeless figures, files, and statistics, could never measure the depth of hurt and outrage dealt out to those of us who love this land. It is because we are Canadians that we protest the violation of our birthright."

Muriel Kitagawa, an internee, writing to the Custodian of Enemy Property, 1943

food, toilet facilities, and medical help. Most families had to stay in these assembly camps for months before being moved.

The journey for Japanese evacuees was not over. Several months after being taken to the makeshift assembly centers, they were told to pack again for their trip to the permanent camps. Most of these camps were east of the Rocky Mountains and well away from the Pacific Coast.

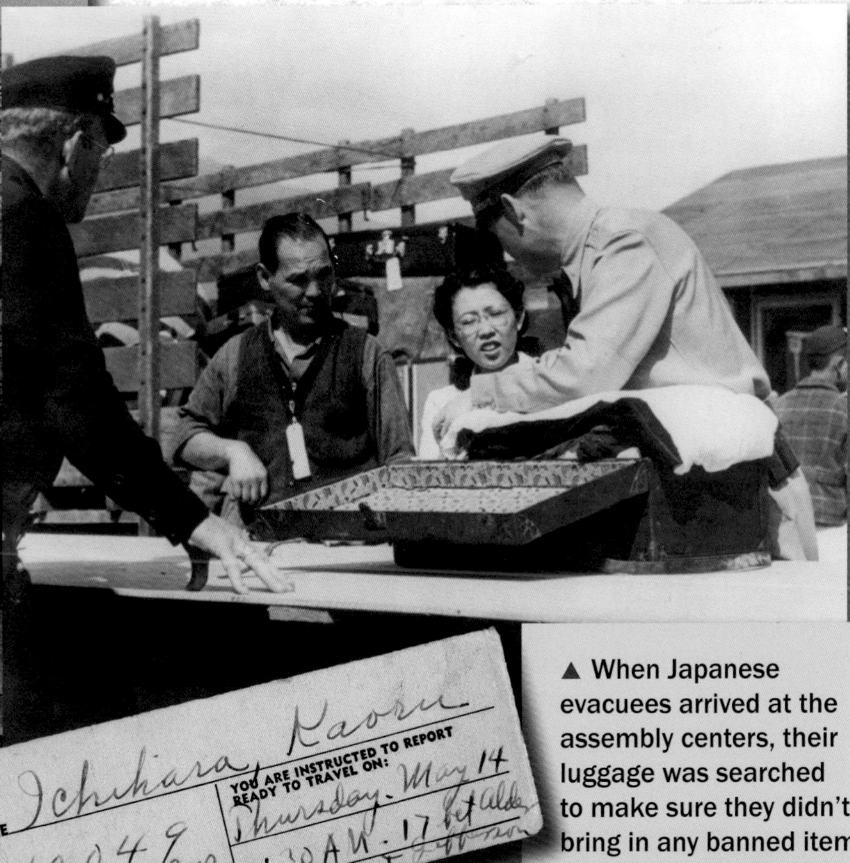

▲ When Japanese evacuees arrived at the assembly centers, their luggage was searched to make sure they didn't bring in any banned items such as weapons.

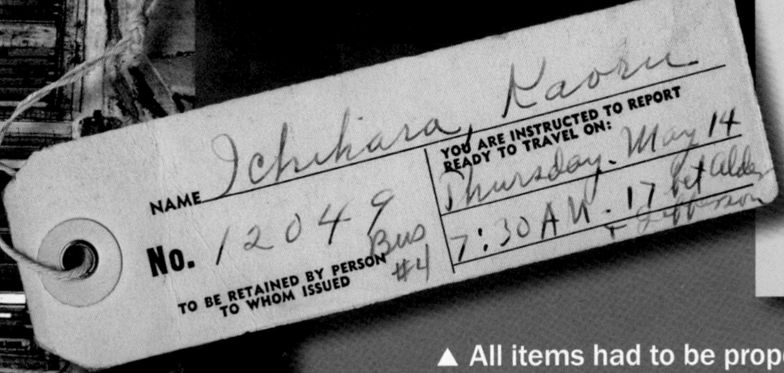

NAME Ichihara Kaoru

No. 12049

YOU ARE INSTRUCTED TO REPORT READY TO TRAVEL ON:

Thursday. May 14

7:30 A.M. 17 Pet Alder

Bus #4

TO BE RETAINED BY PERSON TO WHOM ISSUED

▲ All items had to be properly tied and marked with the name and number of the owner on a tag, like this one belonging to Kaoru Ichihara.

CAMP LIFE

When the internees arrived at the permanent relocation camps, they saw an entirely different landscape. In Canada, ghost towns and farmland in the Slocan Valley in British Columbia became new settlements. In the United States, Manzanar in California and Heart Mountain in Wyoming were just two of ten relocation centers.

At Manzanar, families lived in large tarpaper barracks, divided into "apartments" by cloth **partitions.** Each block had a mess hall for meals and a recreation hall for activities. Internees also built churches and set up schools for the children. The hardest part for internees was the lack of privacy. **Latrines** had no partitions and the showers had no stalls. The camp was surrounded by a high, barbed-wire fence to prevent internees escaping.

In the New Denver camp, families were housed in one-family or two-family cottages. The houses had no insulation and only a small stove for heat and cooking. In smaller camps like Lemon Creek, there was one large building for a school that taught grades K to 12. And while the camps weren't surrounded by barbed-wire, the people were just as isolated and confined.

"... a grave injustice was done to both citizens and permanent resident aliens of Japanese ancestry by the evacuation, relocation, and internment of civilians during World War II."

Statement of Congress, Civil Liberties Act of 1988

▲ The front page of the *Los Angeles Times* on V-J (Victory over Japan) Day, August 15, 1945, welcomed the return of peace.

◄ As the war went on, some children of Japanese-Americans were allowed to serve in the U.S. military. They visited with friends and family at the internment camps when they were on leave. Internees tried to keep life as normal as possible with dances and other social events. The Japanese-Americans in this photograph came from the 442nd Combat Team, whose infantry regiment became the most decorated unit in U.S. military history.

What many internees didn't know was that while they were in the camps the government was selling off their property and possessions. In Canada, the government sold homes, boats, and property at bargain prices. They left the internees with next to nothing. When the war ended, Japanese-Canadians thought they could go back to their old lives. But this was not the case. They had lost everything they had owned and they were not welcome back on the West Coast for years. Internees had only two choices: settle east of the Rockies or move to war-torn Japan.

In the United States, Japanese-Americans were allowed to return to their former towns or settle somewhere new. They had lost all the money and property they had worked years to build up. Now they were living in poverty again. They found that the attitudes of the war against them lingered. Many companies would not hire Japanese-Americans. They had to start all over again.

PERSPECTIVES

Look at the storeowner in this image. Do you think he is concerned about losing business by having a racist sign on his cash register? How do you know?

▶ Many people harbored deep resentment against the Japanese even after the war was over.

WE DON'T WANT ANY JAPS BACK HERE-- EVER!

EVIDENCE REVISITED

"In 1942, my wife and our four children were whipped away from our home . . . all our possessions were left . . . for mother nature to destroy. . . . I tried to pretend it was really a dream and this could not happen to me and my dear family."

Bill Tcheripanoff, Sr., of Akutan in the Aleutian Islands

The Aleutian Islands are a chain of volcanic islands westward from Alaska in the Bering Sea. During World War II, the Japanese invaded two of the islands: Attu and Kiska. They captured the residents and sent them to prisoner-of-war camps back in Japan. The U.S. government quickly insisted that the residents of the remaining islands move to internment camps on mainland Alaska.

Interviews with surviving internees tell us that the Aleuts were given no choice in the matter and were evacuated very quickly. As with the Japanese, they could take only one suitcase each. They were crammed onto ships and, as they sailed away, they watched the military burn their homes and church. The military did not want to leave behind anything that would help the invading Japanese.

Primary source material from the government gives a very **optimistic** view of the relocation of the Aleuts. A report on October 3, 1942, from the superintendent of Alaska Indian Service states that "all of these groups are making a very good adjustment and are all appreciative of the assistance being given to them."

Interviews with former internees tell a different story. Philemon Tutiakoff remembers: "The overcrowded conditions were an **abomination**. There were 28 of us forced to live in one . . . house. There existed no church, no school, no medical facility, no store, no community facility, no [boats], no fishing gear, and no hunting rifles."

ANALYZE THIS

In what ways were the experiences of the Aleuts similar to that of the interned Japanese? In what ways were they different?

▲ U.S. military forces land on one of the Aleutian islands. They brought men and equipment to prepare a counter attack against the Japanese and regain the islands of Kiska and Attu.

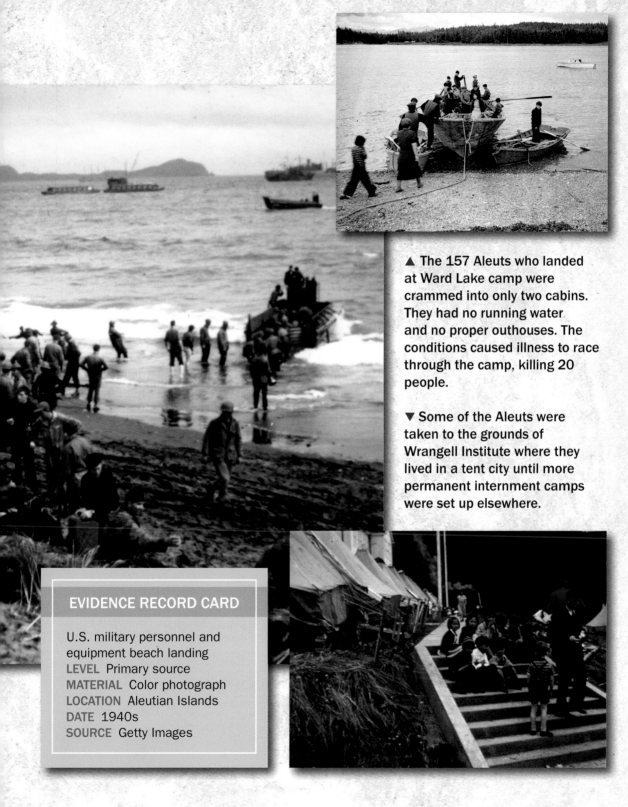

▲ The 157 Aleuts who landed at Ward Lake camp were crammed into only two cabins. They had no running water and no proper outhouses. The conditions caused illness to race through the camp, killing 20 people.

▼ Some of the Aleuts were taken to the grounds of Wrangell Institute where they lived in a tent city until more permanent internment camps were set up elsewhere.

EVIDENCE RECORD CARD

U.S. military personnel and equipment beach landing
LEVEL Primary source
MATERIAL Color photograph
LOCATION Aleutian Islands
DATE 1940s
SOURCE Getty Images

OTHER ENEMY ALIENS

During World War II, not just the Japanese were considered enemy aliens. With the Allies fighting Germans and Italians in Europe, people with these nationalities in North America were viewed with mistrust and suspicion. Governments insisted that these people be interned to "protect" the nation against **sabotage** and spying.

After Canada declared war with Germany in 1939 and Italy in 1940, 26 internment camps were set up across the country. Unlike the 20,000 Japanese-Canadians interned, only about 850 Germans and 600 Italians were sent to the camps. Thousands of others were named "enemy aliens" and had to register and check in with authorities regularly, but were able to continue on with their lives.

In 1940, there were about 1.2 million people who had been born in Germany but were living in the United States. When the United States joined the war in December 1941, the government interned about 11,000 German-Americans as compared to the 120,000 or more Japanese-Americans.

Researchers believe that there was a lower percentage of Germans and Italians in internment camps because the governments was **selective** about who they interned. They looked for people with ties to the Nazis or to **fascist** groups.

While primary sources show the governments producing reports on German spies and members of the Nazi Party, letters from interned Germans to friends or government officials paint a different picture. They were confused and frightened. They didn't understand why they were being questioned and imprisoned. They couldn't learn what charges had led to their arrest or why they were being sent away. "In a concentration camp, I saw rich and poor thrown together in a pit of hell," wrote Italian internee Emilio Galardo in 1940.

◀ The German American Bund organization parades down streets in New York City in 1939. Their aim was to promote a positive view of the Nazi Germany.

HE'S WATCHING YOU

▶ This anti-German poster was meant to warn Americans of the danger of the German Nazis. Images like this heightened the fear of German-Americans.

"We haven't the remotest idea why they arrested him or what's going to happen to him and the many others there. And they won't let me see anyone to find out the charges against him or to do any explaining. Heidi wakes up at nite (sic) screaming 'Papi, papi' and today is Ingrid's first birthday."

Starr Pait Gurcke, wife of American-German internee, July 1942

WANTING TO REMEMBER, WANTING TO FORGET

Internment during World War II was a **traumatic** and **controversial** event for thousands of people. Many Americans and Canadians of Japanese descent were already citizens of their new home country and could not believe that they were being treated like enemies of the state. Their time in the camps made them feel confused, angry, and betrayed by their governments.

Some people strongly believe it is important for them to tell the story of what happened to them in the internment camps. They don't like the idea that this moment in history might be swept under the carpet or forgotten. By telling their stories, they want to expose the fact that these camps were a violation of people's rights. They don't want it to happen to another group of people.

The bigger concern they want to address is that most of society takes its rights for granted. When asked why she was telling her story, Topaz intern Chizu Liyama said: "We learned we have to fight for civil rights."

The former director of the War Relocation Authority, Milton Eisenhower, also felt it was important to remember what happened. He wrote about the camps in his memoirs and stated that he "brooded about this" event because it showed how "society can somehow plunge off course."

Other people find it too painful to discuss what happened. Some, like Bess Chin, don't want to remember and need to block parts of it out. When asked how much she remembered about the trip to the camp in Heart Mountain, Wyoming, she says: "Not much because I didn't want to remember."

▲ Many Japanese-Americans have clear memories of lining up for food in the camps like this one at the Manzanar Relocation Center near Owens Valley, California, in 1943.

"*So as I think back, I think why I can't write about it was because the whole experience of being put into a place like that was traumatic. Being with a family like that was traumatic, and losing all my friends. So, I think this is why I find it extremely difficult to write about that time.*"

Bess K. Chin, former internee, May 17, 2006

PERSPECTIVES

These photographs of life at Manzanar Relocation Center were taken by the famed photographer Ansel Adams, who was hired by the camp director, Ralph Merritt. Adams admitted he was banned from taking certain photos such as of the guard towers and latrines. Do you think there is bias in these photographs? Do you think the smiling Japanese accurately represent what life in the camp was like? Why or why not?

▼ There was no running water in camp houses. Small appliances like a kettle or toaster allowed internees to make light snacks but their main meals were eaten in the mess hall.

"When I think about it now, I have this grateful feeling towards these teachers that came from the outside. Can you imagine that some people pointed to them and said 'Jap lovers' and they couldn't understand why they would spend time in camp trying to teach enemy kids."

Marvin Uratsu, former internee, May 9, 2007

REBUILDING LIVES

Internees released from camps after the war ended faced many challenges. Their property and possessions left behind had been sold or taken. Their businesses had closed and their wealth gone. Starting over meant finding a new place to live and a way to earn money.

Organizations developed that worked to keep the **prejudice** and racism against the Japanese alive. One was the Remember Pearl Harbor League, which formed during the war. Its members were determined to keep the Japanese from returning to resettle along the coast. In an open letter to ministers they stated that: "The Japanese were a menace to these very harbors and our ships when General DeWitt ordered them evacuated: They still are!"

As hard as some groups tried to exclude or deport the Japanese who were now free from the camps, other groups worked just as hard to help them. Church groups like the United Church Ministry set up hotels and hostels in some cities to give returning internees a place to live until they got back on their feet. Debates sprung up in newspapers over the actions of government officials to object to the return of Japanese citizens. Julie Legg, a writer for the *University of Washington Daily* newspaper, wrote: "Here would be a great chance for our

▼ Japanese in propaganda posters were usually portrayed as buck-toothed, nearsighted, and childlike in order to give the impression that they were no match for the Americans fighting them.

" It is the government's plan to get these people out of [British Columbia] as fast as possible. It is my personal intention, as long as I remain in public life, to see they never come back here."

Ian MacKenzie, Canadian federal cabinet minister, 1942

state to take the lead and see that these loyal Americans are given just treatment."

In Canada, it took until 1949—four years after the war was over—for all restrictions to be lifted from Japanese-Canadians. Almost 4,000 had already been deported to Japan. The rest were free to return to the West Coast, but by then there was no home to return to. "It can never be as it was before," said Mary Murakami on her return to Salt Spring Island, British Columbia.

PERSPECTIVES

Take a close look at this photo of the lunch counter Mr. and Mrs. Yamamoto opened after their internment. Who do you think most of their customers were? Do you think they are doing well in their new business? Give your reasons.

▼ The Yamamotos had lived in Los Angeles for more than 20 years before they were interned at the Gila Relocation Center. After their release, they opened a lunch counter specializing in native Japanese dishes.

HISTORY REPEATED

"We cannot change the past. But we must, as a nation, have the courage to face up to these historical facts."

Brian Mulroney,
Canadian prime minister, 1988

In looking back at the events surrounding internment camps of World War II, what have we learned? Will governments in times of war or terrorism again strip citizens of their civil rights because of fear and racism? Will the general population and human rights organizations allow such extreme measures to be used?

Even during World War II when the idea of internment camps was discussed, some people tried to look at the situation objectively and reasonably. Major-General Ken Stuart of the Canadian Army said: "From the army point of view, I cannot see that Japanese-Canadians constitute the slightest menace to national security." But his voice was not heard, and the internment of Japanese-Canadians went forward.

Both Canadian and American governments have now issued formal apologies and offered **restitution** to surviving internees. In Canada, the War Measures Act that gave the government the right to intern groups indefinitely was **repealed.** In its place is the Emergencies Act. It differs from the War Measures Act in that any temporary laws made under the act have to fit with the Charter of Rights and Freedoms.

In the United States, several of the camp locations have been preserved as historical landmarks. Congress said this was to "stand as reminders that this nation failed in its most sacred duty to protect its citizens against prejudice, greed, and political expediency."

▼ Tashme camp in British Columbia was the biggest Japanese-Canadian internment camp, holding about 2,600 internees. It was also the most isolated, not near any town or any other camp.

▲ Andy Noguchi participates in an interfaith service during a recent Manzanar pilgrimage at the Manzanar Historic Site in the Owens Valley, California. Noguchi, who helped organize the **pilgrimage**, had two uncles who were interned at Manzanar internment camp as orphans during World War II.

ANALYZE THIS

Looking back at the context of the bombing of Pearl Harbor and the war against Japan, do you think concerns about "enemy aliens" and the idea of internment camps were reasonable? Why or why not?

TODAY'S ENEMY ALIENS

Since WWII, prejudice and racism in North America against people of Japanese origin seems to have lessened. But other groups of people are becoming the focus of the same fear and hate.

Because of terrorist attacks around the world by **extremists,** a new group of people has become a target for discrimination. Muslims are people who follow the religion of Islam. They are identified by their faith. Extremists of this religion have carried out horrific attacks around the world.

Suspicion and mistrust skyrocketed against Muslims after the terrorist attacks of 9/11. This is similar to the increase in anti-Japanese feelings following an incident in Hawaii some hours after the attack on Pearl Harbor. A Japanese pilot who had participated in that attack crash-landed his plane on the Hawaiian Island of Ni'ihau. There, three men of Japanese heritage helped the pilot find weapons and take hostages. This event kickstarted the internment of Japanese-Americans.

The same mistrust is applied to Muslims. After the 9/11 attacks, Muslim mosques were **vandalized** and Muslims have been harassed and threatened. Some people think they are secretly helping the terrorists. They question their loyalty. They dislike the cultural differences. They have not interned Muslims, but many places in the world are turning back refugees because they are Muslims. Those who have been through the times of internment of Japanese, Germans, Italians, Ukrainians, and Jews wonder if we will repeat our mistakes because we have forgotten the past.

> ### ANALYZE THIS
>
> How is the situation with Muslim discrimination today similar to what happened with Japanese people during World War II? How is it different?

"I really think that if people would just get out there and talk to a Muslim person, they would see that they are human just like you. We're just as upset about what's going on and how people are being hurt. It's devastating to us as well."

Terry Cormier, *The Washington Post*, December 3, 2015

► Thousands joined in this protest march on International Women's Day in Toronto, Ontario. One of the themes was raising awareness about racial discrimination.

Down With Islamophobia! — No to Harper-CSIS Surveillance State!

◄ Some people believe the U.S. naval base in Guantanamo Bay, Cuba, is a modern-day concentration camp. The internees, like these Muslims, are held without charges or a trial.

TIMELINE

1768 First use of the term "concentration camp," being used in Poland during the Bar Confederation Rebellion

1907 Anti-Asian riot in Vancouver, B.C.

1921 Asiatic Exclusion League is formed

1939 Start of World War II. Canada declares war on Germany

1942 Nazis begin building "extermination" or "death" camps, where prisoners are gassed

March 16, 1942 First Japanese-Canadians arrive at Hasting Park Assembly Center

March 25, 1942 Japanese-Canadians begin being moved to internment camps in the interior

August 10, 1942 First Japanese-American internees are moved to internment camps

August 14, 1945 The surrender of Japan ends the war in the Pacific

October 15, 1945 All internment camps in the United States except Tule Lake are closed

1768

1900

1941

1945

1877 First Japanese immigrant lands and settles in Victoria, B.C.

1914 World War I begins. Canada interns Germans, Ukrainians, and Bulgarians among others

1933 First Nazi concentration camp, Dachau, Germany, opened to hold political prisoners and union organizers

December 7, 1941 Japan attacks Pearl Harbor

February 18, 1942 President Roosevelt signs Executive Order 9066

March 18, 1942 The War Relocation Authority is formed

March 31, 1942 Japanese-Americans begin arriving at Assembly Centers

May 7, 1945 The surrender of Germany ends the war in Europe

September 2, 1945 All internment camps in Canada except New Denver are ordered closed and destroyed

March 20, 1946 Last internment camp in the United States (Tule Lake) closes

March 31, 1949 All restrictions finally lifted from Japanese-Canadians

1946

September 17, 1987 Civil Liberties Act passed in the United States offering acknowledgment and payments to internment camp survivors

September 22, 1988 Canada acknowledges, apologizes, and offers compensation to surviving Canadian internees

1994 In Canada, New Denver Historic Site opens at the former internment camp

1994

Japanese internment camps in the United States and Canada

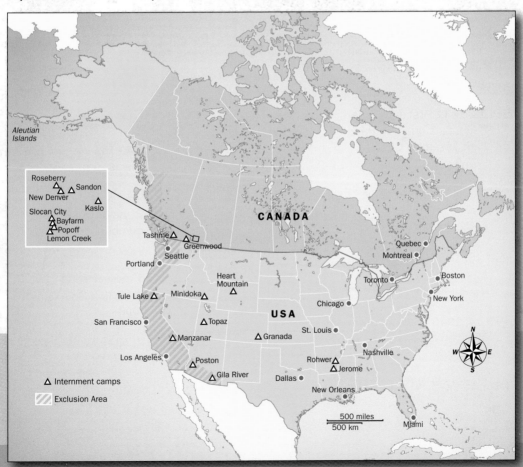

BIBLIOGRAPHY

QUOTATIONS AND EXCERPTS

p. 4 Robert Penn Warren: *The Legacy of the Civil War,* Bison Books, 1998.

p. 6 Roosevelt, Franklin D., Executive Order No. 9066, February 19, 1942.

p. 8 Courtney Sato: New Sterling Library Exhibit, *Yale News*, November 2, 2015.

p. 11 Chin, Bess K. Audio interview: www.tellingstories.org/internment/bchin/index.html

p. 15 Uchida, Yoshiko. *The Bracelet*. Puffin Books, 1996.

p. 16 John Adams: *The History of the Rise, Progress and Establishment of the Independence of the United States*, Vol. 1, p. 296, Dilly, London, 1788.

p. 18 Nightingale, E. C. "Attack at Pearl Harbor, 1941." EyeWitness to History, www.eyewitnesstohistory.com 1997.

p. 20 Henry McLemore: Hearst newspapers, January 29, 1942.

p. 22 The Young China Club poster: http://bit.ly/25c6EVj

p. 24 The Alien Registration Act: www.citizensource.com/History/20thCen/Smith.htm

p. 26 Kitagawa, Muriel. Letter to the Custodian of Enemy Property, 1943. https://canadianjapaneseinternmentcamps.wordpress.com

p. 28 Statement of Congress, Civil Liberties Act, 1988.

p. 30 Bill Tcheripanoff, Sr., Aleutian/Pribilof Island Association, National Archives. http://bc-inc–1.empowernetwork.com/blog/aleut-evacuation

p. 30 Vanasse, Deb. *Picture This, Alaska: Historic Photographs from the Last Frontier*, p. 126. ReadHowYouWant, 2011.

pp. 32/33 Gurcke, Starr Pait. Memorial University Libraries Document Archives. http://site.gaic.info/wp-content/uploads/2016/01/Costa-Rica_July-1942_jpg.pdf

p. 34 Chin, Bess K. Audio interview: www.tellingstories.org/internment/bchin/index.html

p. 35 Uratsu, Marvin. Audio interview: www.tellingstories.org/internment/muratsu/index.html

p. 36 Mackenzie, Ian. *The Province*, April 4, 1942.

p. 38 Brian Mulroney: House of Commons, September 22, 1988.

p. 40 Cormier, Terry. *The Washington Post*, December 3, 2015.

WEBSITES AND MULTIMEDIA

Audio interviews with transcripts from former Japanese internees at Telling Their Stories: **www.tellingstories.org/internment/index.html**

The true story of Japanese Canadian internee Irene Tsuyuki: **www.whitepinepictures.com/seeds/i/8/sidebar.html**

Read the letters and postcards school children who were Japanese internees sent their librarian Miss Breed: **www.janm.org/exhibits/breed/title.htm**

PBS gives insight into Children of the Camps, including documents and a timeline: **www.pbs.org/childofcamp/history**

INTERNET GUIDELINES

Finding good source material on the Internet can sometimes be a challenge. When analyzing how reliable the information is, consider these points:

- Who is the author or creator of the page? Is it an expert in the field or a person who experienced the event?
- Is the site well known and up-to-date? A page that has not been updated for several years probably has out-of-date information.
- Can you verify the facts with another site? Always double-check information.
- Have you checked all possible sites? Don't just look on the first page a search engine provides. Remember to try government sites and research papers.
- Have you recorded website addresses and names? Keep this data so you can backtrack and verify the information you want to use.

The History Channel's video about Japanese-American internment: **www.history.com/topics/world-war-ii/japanese-american-relocation**

Audio file by the History Channel of 1943 radio broadcast by Dillon S. Meyer, director of the War Relocation Authority, on his disapproval of Japanese internment: **http://bit.ly/1T3RQmV**

TO FIND OUT MORE

Non-fiction:
Cooper, Michael. *Remembering Manzanar*. New York, Clarion, 2002.

Hickman, Pamela and Fukawa, Masako. *Righting Canada's Wrongs: Japanese Canadian Internment in the Second World War*. Toronto, ON, James Lorimer, 2012.

Oppenheim, Joanne. *Dear Miss Breed*. New York, Scholastic, 2006.

Stanley, Jerry. *I Am an American: A True Story of Japanese Internment*. New York, Scholastic, 1998.

Tunnell, Michael O. and Chilcoat, George W. *The Children of Topaz*. New York, Holiday House, 1996.

Uchida, Yoshiko. *The Invisible Thread*. Englewood Cliffs, NJ, J. Messner, 1991.

Historical fiction:
Bunting, Eve. *So Far from the Sea*. New York, HMH Books for Young Readers, 2009.

Denenberg, Barry. *My Name is America: The Journal of Ben Uchida*. New York, Scholastic, 2003.

Kadohata, Cynthia. *Weedflower*. New York, Atheneum Books for Young Readers, 2009.

Uchida, Yoshiko. *The Bracelet*. New York, Puffin Books, 1996.

GLOSSARY

abomination A thing that causes disgust or hatred

accurate Correct in all details; true to the situation

accused A person charged with a crime or wrongdoing

Aleuts People living on the Aleutian Islands near Alaska

analyze To examine something in detail in order to explain or understand it

artifact An object made by a human, usually with cultural or historical significance

auditory sources Source material that you can hear, such as speech

bias Not being completely fair or objective; favoring one thing over another

Bias Rule A guideline for writing history that says historians should think about each piece of evidence critically

civilians Ordinary citizens of a country; those who do not belong to a military or police force

concentration camp A prison or detention center used during wartime

confine Keep someone within certain limits

conquering To take control using military force

context The circumstances or setting in which an event happens

controversial Likely to cause public disagreement

critically Using careful judgment

culture The ideas, customs, and behavior of a people

death camps Concentration camps used by the Germans in World War II to kill Jews and other enemies of the state

detention Being held or delayed, for example in an internment camp

discrimination Unjust treatment of people based on race or religion

ephemera Things that are important for a short time

evacuation Emptying out

evaluating Forming an idea about

evidence Information or facts that indicate whether something is true

extremists People who resort to extreme or severe actions

facist A believer or follower of fascism

forcibly Done with force; against people's wishes

immigrants People who come to live in another country

interned Confined or held against your wishes for political or military reasons

name for a concentration camp

interpretations Explanations

justified Declared to be right

latrines Outhouses

memoirs Writings based on people's personal histories

mentality A way of thinking

Nazi Party An extreme political party—of National Socialist Workers—that ruled Germany from 1933 to 1945

objective Without bias or prejudice

optimistic Hopeful

partitions Dividing walls

patriotic Supporting your own country

pilgrimage Journey of a religious person to a sacred place

prejudice Negative opinions not based on fact

preserved Kept in its original state

primary source A firsthand memory, account, document, or artifact from the past that serves as a historical record about what happened at a particular time

racism Prejudice against someone of a different race

repealed Reversed a law

restitution Compensate for injury or loss

restrictions Limits on being able to doing something

sabotage Damaging or destroying something on purpose

secondary source A historian's or artist's interpretation of a primary source

selective Choosing carefully

sinister Evil and frightening

source material Original document or other piece of evidence

temporary For a short while

traumatic Very distressing

vandalized Destroyed on purpose

visual Having to do with the sense of sight

World War I War fought from 1914 to 1918 between the United States, Canada, the United Kingdom, France, Italy, Japan, and their allies against Germany, Austria-Hungary, Bulgaria, and Ottoman Turkey and their allies; the United States did not enter the war until 1917

World War II War fought from 1939 to 1945 between the United States, Canada, Britain, France, the U.S.S.R. and their allies against Nazi Germany, Italy, Japan, and their allies; the U.S.S.R., United States, and Japan did not join the war until 1941

INDEX